BEATING THE ODDS

HOW JESUS SAVED MY LIFE

WRITTEN BY

THOMAS C. HIGHTOWER

Beating the Odds, How Jesus saved my Life
by Thomas C. Hightower

Interior Book Design and Layout by
www.integrativeink.com

ISBN: 978-1-7337562-1-1

This book is dedicated to my beautiful daughters,
Gianna and Ava Hightower.

CONTENTS

PROLOGUE

Definition of Odds: "The ratio between the amounts staked by the parties to a bet, based on the expected probability either way. The chances or likelihood of something happening or being the cause. Superiority in strength, power, or resources; advantage" (dictionary.com).

In 2005, many life changes were happening to me. I just graduated from Norfolk State University and decided to move west for a new beginning. My journey was long and I traveled cross country in my white '91 Nissan Sentra, which had only two hubcaps. Traveling west was the start of a new life and a goal of mine prior to graduation.

While living in Phoenix, Arizona, I was twenty-four years old and had a vision of writing a book about my life. For the last ten years, I have been battling with a need to express myself through words and, ultimately, leave behind a legacy that no one could misconstrue. The purpose of this book isn't to offend or hurt anyone, especially in my immediate family. Every word, every thought, has been backed with unconditional love. Today, I am at a place in my life where God is in the center of my thoughts and reason. I want to share life lessons, as well as triumphs and defeats, to illustrate to my audience that anything is possible in life when God is followed. Learn from my mistakes, and learn from my success.

I am not a perfect man; however, I am a man who tries his best. I want my audience to walk away knowing that even with adversity and pain, they, too, can succeed in this thing called life. We are all on an equal playing field, in my opinion. In this life, it is guaranteed that we will hurt, suffer, bleed, and even cry at least once. We are not victims of this reality; in fact, we are all made greater because of it. Before we take our first breath, we are fighting for our lives. Up to a hundred million sperm fight to enter a woman's egg and only one will succeed. Before we enter this world, the odds are already stacked against us!

When you walk with me through this journey, please hold tight to my hand. If you are a friend, a family member, or even a stranger, please know one thing: I love you with all my heart. Thank you for taking the time to accompany me on this journey. I invite you into my soul—not to agree with all my thoughts but just to understand where I came from. Be open-minded to the words I write. I still share a lot of pain from an overwhelming divorce, unemployment, and a constant fight with heavy depression. I don't seek sympathy or recognition; I seek only the truth through my expression. What you do with these words is entirely up to you. Words are powerful when used with love. My goal is for my audience to see that hope and God are real energies. Know that no matter how hard your life gets, you can still overcome, as I did.

Now, with all that said, grab my hand, and let's start on this memorable journey.

It began on April 11, 1981 in Hartford, Connecticut....

WHISPERS IN THE AIR

Jesus reminds us that through suffering love is born
No need to hold grudges or even to feel scorn
I thank God for all the things that have happened in life
Even though I am single, no longer with a wife
I have become a better man, more forgiving man to
those who speak hate
No longer in fear of being great
Yes, I made mistakes in my life and some judge me blind
I forgive those who judge my shameful past
Eventually they will unveil their sinister mask
I speak out of love to those who want me destroyed
In my dreams, I hear their disrespect and when
they called me little boy
Pompous, parasite, and even a bad man
As long as I have God, I must take a positive stand
I love you all for opening my big, brown eyes
Be careful of friends and people you think you might despise
Before I close my eyes, please know I live without fear
Understand the wisdom of whispers in the air

CHAPTER 1

CHILDHOOD

I was born April 11, 1981, at Hartford Hospital in Hartford, Connecticut. My parents were Nellie Sgarellino and Eddie Hightower. Eddie had his own family, and I was cultivated from an affair. I would only see my father in the flesh two times my entire life.

My first memory of childhood was when I was four years old. The memory of that day went like this:

"Mommy, Mommy, I can't sleep," I said, speaking to her from the top of the stairs.

"Boy, you'd better go to bed. It's midnight," my mother said from the living room, while rocking in her chair.

I walked down the stairs. "Why are you up, Mom?"

My mother still rocked in her rocking chair. "Because I can't sleep either," she said.

My mother worked three jobs trying to support the three of us, and I could see the pain in her eyes even at four years old. She was tired, lonely, and angry at the world. We were all four years apart in age—Alex and Chrissy were my older siblings. Alex was twelve at the time, and Chrissy was eight.

At times, we were on welfare, and my mother did her very best supporting three children. I was the youngest for the longest time, so I grew up pretty fast. My sister and I were the closest because my older brother spent his time experiencing life as a teenager in the city.

We grew up in the north end on Lebanon Street. The city consisted of Black, Puerto Rican, and other nationalities. Hartford had its share of gangs and is in between two major cities: New York and Boston. It was not all good and was a place my mother strived hard to leave due to increasing crime and other things I will discuss later.

Our family make-up was extremely complex. All of my siblings had different fathers, and we were all bi-racial, except for my mother. Mom was a first-generation Italian, and my grandparents came all the way from Melilli, Sicily—a place I would later find out was a small village and still battered by WWII in some areas.

My father already had his own family, and he would get my mother pregnant only to sell her a dream of creating a family with her—at least, that's what I was told. Those lies would eventually come out as I got older.

I was a skinny, mixed kid who didn't know his father, and really didn't know my identity at a young age. Mom did her very best to give us the best life, and looking back, I don't know how she did it. She was a strong and courageous woman. Alex was the man of the house, a phenomenal athlete and a handsome kid. I give my brother a lot of credit, having the responsibility that he had at age twelve.

In my opinion, his childhood would suffer some due to the increase in adult responsibilities.

We would go watch him play football and see him glide through the wind with his daring speed. At a very young age, I remember wanting to be just like him—and even better. He introduced me to sports at five years old, and I credit him for showing me how cool sports were. I would adopt professional teams like the New York Giants and the New York Yankees because those were his favorite teams. Whatever my brother admired, so did I. He truly was my idol.

By the age of six, I was obsessed with sports. Every single day, I would play football, basketball, and challenge the kids in the neighborhood to competitive races. Winning was everything in our house, even though we didn't have an abundance of things. All of us competed in organized sports, and all of us were pretty good—meaning we stood out. I knew when I was young that I would go on and be special in sports because I loved to compete so much.

A funny story from my home on Lebanon Street was the chipmunk story. We used to have an old refrigerator outside, on the side of our duplex, and this chipmunk lived inside of it. I would get home from school, see the chipmunks sitting on top of the refrigerator, and I would throw rocks at them. One day, I actually hit the chipmunks with a rock. The squirrel ran down the refrigerator, and I would run from *him*, crying and peeing my pants. This could be how my running career started but ironically, I no longer like chipmunks.

Grandpa and Grandma would come to some of our games, and we enjoyed showing them our talents. They would also visit us during the holidays and see us from time to time, along with my aunt, who lived with them. They lived in Middletown, Connecticut, which at the time was heavily populated with Italian immigrants. It was a small town where everyone knew eachother and the restaurants were incredible.

I always had great respect for my grandparents and wish I'd spent more time with them. Grandma Gloria was a house wife and one of the best cooks on the planet. When I had the opportunity to visit, I would spend hours in the kitchen just watching her cook. She would make bread from scratch and make all her sauces from scratch, too. I always wanted her recipes, but she would tell me, "They are all in my head."

My grandparents were an odd couple from what I saw because my grandfather was very active outside of the house, and my grandmother was confined to the inside. I would later find out my grandmother didn't even have a driver's license, and back then it was common for a wife to just look after the home. In Italy, that's how it was.

Grandma Gloria carried a lot of anger. I wasn't aware of the source of that anger until later in life, when I became older and began asking questions. Her father molested her at a very young age. She would keep it secret until she was forty-three years old. I learned about this from other family members after her death. Her anger, at times, was a lot—especially seeing it as a kid—but I didn't judge her and still had an abundant amount of love for her regardless.

Grandpa was a handsome man, with a deep, Italian voice. At times it was very hard to understand him unless you stood very close to him. His English was not as polished as my grandmother's. He was a hard worker who spent many years in the factories. His hard work and savings allowed him to purchase a car and house. When he wasn't working, I remember seeing him in beautiful suits and always looking sharp.

In addition to being a hard worker, he was also active at an Italian social club called the garibaldis. This group of Italian men met once a week, and my grandfather eventually became the president of the club. As a child, when I visited the club, all the men looked so serious to me because they all spoke Italian. As a kid, I admired the way they dressed and how they carried themselves as men.

When my grandparents argued, they would speak Italian, and the conflicts were intense. After arguing, my grandfather would go to his garden for hours and smoke his cigarettes and clean up his garden. His garden would provide a significant amount of food for their family. Watching my grandfather garden planted the seeds in my mind to also want to garden later in life.

They would have two daughters only, and my aunt plus my mother would turn out to be complete opposites. Auntie Phyllis was reserved and quiet, and my mother always had a big mouth and loved confrontation. Back then, Italians and African Americans did not generally get along, so my mother having interracial relationships was not well looked upon. Outside of my grandparents, I really didn't know my Italian side of the family. I always felt as if we were a bit outcast.

I would be introduced to Catholic church because my grandma loved to go on Sundays. My mother wasn't a church goer, so we only went when we saw our grandparents. Church was not my cup of tea—especially Catholic church. It was long and boring, for the most part, and very formal. I remember enjoying the donuts at the end of service, and oddly my grandfather was always there at the end to pick us up. He was not present in the church with us, though.

My brother began getting into a lot of trouble in the city, so we moved to Manchester, Connecticut. Manchester was outside of Hartford but not as busy as Hartford. When we arrived in Manchester, we would watch my brother stand out from the other kids and take off in football.

We were always home alone during the day because my mother was working her tail off with multiple jobs. This meant we were unsupervised a lot of the time and were introduced to many things kids should not be introduced to. By the age of eight, I lost my virginity, and that would affect the way I was in every relationship. Certain things that were going on around me became normal before I was even ten years old. Sex, drugs, and doing bad things in the neighborhood were norms.

Alex was in charge of keeping an eye on us, but at this point he was a teenager and doing his own thing with his friends. We would walk to school and most of the time do crazy things, such as throw rocks at cars and then run. Chrissy was my guardian most of the time, and we spent a lot of time together. She always looked out for me and had my back. I think that's why to this day I feel like I understand women so much. I learned so much from her.

While in Manchester, my mother began dating a white man, and we did not pay much attention at first. He was shy, and we all thought he was out of his mind because we were all pretty crazy. Tim was a hard-working man who met my mother while at work. He was a lot younger than her, and as blue collar as they come. His family was living in a place called Stafford Springs, Connecticut. We would go there every now and then for special events to see them. It was in the middle of nowhere in northern Connecticut, right up against the Massachusetts line.

As their relationship grew stronger, and Manchester got worse with crime, my mother uprooted us to Stafford Springs to live right on Main Street. Stafford was a small town of about forty thousand people, predominantly white, and away from city life. There was really no one of color, and everyone knew everyone. I didn't know what to think of it at first because all I cared about was signing up for football and being just like my big brother.

The first kid I met there was Tom Balanceau. He lived across the street in a multi-unit yellow apartment complex, and he loved football, too. His brother Phil would be introduced to me, and we immediately became best friends. Their family was large, and Big Phil and Maureen would become my second family. I would stay the night over there even when Tom and Phil were out of state in New York to visit their other family. I would spend almost every day in their house.

The first time I ever heard the N-word was in third grade at school. A kid called me that, and I remember being so mad that I fought him. I didn't even really understand the word. I just knew it was a bad word. Maureen would sit me down that day and tell me black is beautiful, and I thought it was strange coming from a white lady I barely even knew. She would go on to be a second mother to me, and her husband Phil was like a second father figure.

Mr. Ray Young was another influential man in my life. His son, Mark, and I were best friends, and Ray would make us the best breakfasts during the weekends. In addition to that, he would take Mark and me to several movies and ride bikes with us. They lived right down the street, and I got to see him work hard every day and be a standup role model as a man. When I was out there away from my own home, I was fortunate to have parental figures around me who showed me a lot of positivity. I just loved the families near our house, and they always made me feel like I was part of their family. Living in a small town was really nice, to have that kind of love.

Every single day, the kids in the neighborhood would meet in the church parking lot (it was big) and play tag football. We played as if we were trying out for the NFL, creating championship title games and imitating our favorite pro football players. I would go on to get serious in midget football, and my brother would go into high school as a star running back. I remember everyone asking me if I was Alex Williams' little brother, and it made me feel good. I knew he was popular, and I wanted to have that same recognition someday.

I wanted to use college as my tool to conquer the world. Not one person from my family had achieved such a goal, and my brother would later go into the military, only to forfeit the dream I had for him. My older sister began to rebel and fight constantly with my mother and stepdad. The environment in which I lived was so loud and destructive at times. I just wanted a better life, a life with peace. To this day, I think that's why I am so calm. I don't believe in yelling or screaming to get a point across. Like most families, we had our good days and bad days. I was always appreciated my family, even through the bad times. Those experiences helped mold me into who I am today.

Every day after school, I would go to the basketball court and play at Olympic field. This allowed me to find refuge and peace while playing for hours. When I was alone, it allowed me to get used to trusting myself. I never got in the habit of depending on anyone. In fact, the only person I ever depended on was myself. I was athletic and created a work ethic by playing every single day. Unfortunately, the friends I had were starting to create their own paths for life. Some chased drugs, others chased crime, and others would later die from mistakes they had made.

In the back of my mind, I searched for my father and wondered where he was. Everyone else had a father who would go to the games and be there for them. I wondered why my dad wasn't around. After I had a great game, it would hurt when the fathers of my friends came up to me, congratulating me. It somehow made it worse, getting recognition from other fathers. What had I done to keep my own father away? Some nights, I would stay up thinking that if I became a star maybe then he would come around.

I was never angry at my father, never once. It's odd because most of my pain has come from his lack of being a dad to me. I was always hopeful he would come around, but that hope would slip away the older I became.

As a child, I loved to write poetry and short stories. Many of my friends would later go to jail, so I used to write them a lot. Writing became another way to escape from the pain and release my thoughts.

So there I was: a skinny, bi-racial kid in an all-white town, who didn't know his biological father, and all my siblings had different dads. Talk about an identity crisis! As a child, I was well received by other kids in my school on the surface. But I never felt white, and I never really felt black. I was just Tom Hightower, a loving kid who genuinely loved others and wanted to play. Mentally, I asked a lot of questions to myself, though. Was life really about going to school and then going to work forever? That seemed so boring and unadventurous. I wanted to get out and see the world and help others in the process.

One of the first turning points in my journey was in middle school. I tried out to make the school team in sixth grade. The tryouts consisted of three practices, and after each practice, cuts were made. Only two sixth graders made it to the final practice. Todd B. and I were on the short list, which was taped to the gym wall. Todd was one of my best friends, and we also played rec ball together. I thought for sure we would make it together; however, that would not be the case. Todd would go on and make the team, and I was cut. It was the first time I ever felt defeat in sports, and the pain was so real it still hurts to this day. I was so upset and disappointed. I was happy for Todd, and that did not impact our relationship one bit, but I was on a mission.

Todd's entire family really embraced me with a lot of love and affection. The first time I ever saw big money was over at Todd's father's house. His mom and dad were divorced, so when his dad had him, I would sleep over there. His dad had a cabin house, large swimming pool, and I was blown away how big the house was. Ironically my mother worked at the same company as Todd's father. I wanted a house like that.

Even though I didn't really understand the value of money just yet, sports was my true passion and love. Every day, I practiced sports until 8 pm and remained focused—so much so that nothing else seemed to matter. I was a skinny kid who had trouble getting on the court because of my size. The adults did not want to pick me to be on their team, so many times I had to wait to play later in the night, when the guys were tired. It was so competitive because there were a lot of teams ready to play, and if your team lost, you may not get a chance to get back on the court. I didn't care though. I would watch and watch all night long, shooting and dribbling. The commitment became an obsession all because of a middle school tryout that went bad.

At this point, my brother had gone to the Marine Corps, and my older sister was doing her thing in high school. Drugs and crime became more frequent around me, and life became more complex. I would go on to start working on tobacco fields and take on other jobs that I could get to have my own cash. We all worked at a young age, and sitting around the house was never an option. All of my friends were pretty lost and getting into a lot of trouble, and I was around it all. I was around the consumption of drugs and bad decisions daily. If I was guilty of anything, it was the bad company I kept at times. This wasn't to say I was a saint though because I was involved in the consumption of drug use at times. What could I do though? Even though my friends were making bad decisions with their lives, I couldn't stop being their friend. I never thought I was better than anyone—and still don't even to this day. I have always accepted everyone for who they are, and I thank God for the precious gift of knowing them.

My sister would begin dating guys who were drug dealers, and they became my role models. I had a lot of respect for my sister and I looked up to her. With my brother gone, I gravitated to men who had some money and nice clothes. I was going into clubs and seeing things on the street by the time I was in seventh grade. It was only a matter of time before reality would come knocking right at my door.

The moment I truly found my gift was during middle school, a national fitness test, where we would do push-ups, sit ups, stretching, and running. Our results would be captured, and me being super competitive, I would unveil a talent that would one day be the bridge to my dream—running.

We would run a mile for time, and I would run in basketball shoes and basketball shorts fast and beat everyone easily. I was so fast that the middle school cross-country coach would constantly try to get me to run. I was not going for that one bit. Basketball was my love, and I decided I would never be a sissy runner.

Finally, I caught the attention of the high school's cross-country coach Steve Levinthal. He had won eleven state championships, was a respected coach, and one of the town's legends. He was so much of a legend they even named the street around the school after him—Levinthal Way. He recruited me hard, and I was not trying to hear it. My mother even grounded me until I went to a practice because I'd started to find myself getting into increasing trouble. I didn't care. I knew my friends would pick on me for days if I ran cross-country and track.

Then one day, I was getting out of the shower and heard someone knocking at my door. A group of beautiful girls from the cross-country team were standing there. I was so nervous to answer the door. They were inviting me to a practice, and that's what would finally get me to entertain running. The first practice I went to, I saw girls beautiful and in shape running near the boys team. I was motivated to go to practice to see them.

Coach Leventhal was a master mind. He never taught us how to run fast; he taught us mental toughness. Everything we did had a purpose, and it involved being strong—whether it was screaming during exercising or running unlimited hills after a long practice. The man was a genius! His tactics were clever and unique, and for some reason, he would look at me and tell me all the time, "You are going to be special!" That statement, coming from him, was out of the norm. He never praised runners. At least if he did, I just never heard him do so.

Of course, I thought he was out of his mind because I was just out there to see pretty girls. Running was so easy because those that can endure the most pain succeed. I loved pain, and running was an outlet to express my pain. To see another man ahead of you in pain, and you going around him, psychologically told him you were stronger.

I would go on to make the varsity team, and as a freshman that was a huge honor. Coach always made us believe our efforts weren't good enough. He would push us and push us and at one point, I thought he was crazy. He would throw his clipboard and go home and tell us to figure the shit out on our own. As a team, we were well organized and knew exactly what to do even without him there. Then he'd come back to see what was going on, and he would still be in a rage. Everything he did was mental.

I remember some of the upperclassman being jealous of me running fast, and I was shocked because I didn't care about varsity or being good. They would call me varsity boy when I was a freshman. Running on varsity was a big deal, I guess. Still, I ran just to look at the girls and to use it to get conditioning for basketball, so I really didn't care about the outcome.

We would go on that year (freshman year) to win states by 1 point. Coach Levinthal would have his second heart attack that winter, and he would pass away unexpectedly at the young age of 53 years old. Our cross-country team would never go on to win states again, or even be competitive. I was so upset because he was a big reason why I continued to get faster and start to enjoy running. He taught me things about my mind that would carry me through college athletics. He was a man that had God's gift in coaching and motivating high school kids.

So here I was in high school and a varsity athlete. Here come the girls, the drugs, and the trouble all around me more abundantly. But when coach died, another assistant coach would carry his legacy's message and coach me hard. Her name was Coach Karen. She was a small woman in stature had the heart of a lion. She would motivate me and keep me far away from the ladies. She would help me go on to win class "SS" state championships and win All-Conference honors in track. Coach Karen had a way of getting through to me. On a regular basis, she would say, "Don't you want to get out of here and go to college?" Her words hit home when I was trapped mentally into doing the wrong thing. For some odd reason, I would listen, and winning states in conference was dedicated to her. She kept me in line, and to this day I will always be grateful of our relationship.

So one world was athletics and fun, and the other world was my friends, who were now involving themselves with crime. All I wanted to do was play ball and go to the basketball court. I was experimenting in drinking and smoking weed occasionally. Ironically, I never had a serious girlfriend in high school. Sports were my true love.

When my brother came home to visit, it was hard because he was now a man, and gradually I felt distant towards him. He brought home a charismatic woman whom he would later marry. Her name was Angela Dickerson, and I loved her. She always made me smile. She was a marine, just like my brother, and had an energetic personality. She and my brother were a beautiful couple, and I would be in their wedding as my brother's best man. They would marry in Missouri, in a small town where Angela grew up.

During my high school years, I would see a lot—some good, some bad, and ultimately things that would alter my path. I lost two best friends in high school to death and had other best friends go to jail. All of this happened right in front of my eyes. I knew I had to get out. My grades were bad because I just couldn't sit still in school. I didn't enjoy school because all I could think about was sports. I was never home because I was always at the basketball court after cross-country practice. I would get home around 8:30 every single night. At the basketball court, guys would smoke and drink and get into trouble. I loved it, though, because the older I got, the better my game became.

⁓

Hip hop in the '90s was the golden age of music. I would fall in love with Tupac Shakur, Biggie Smalls, and various other rappers. Rap music played a huge role in my life—artists like the Wu-Tang Clan, Snoop Dogg, Mobb Deep, and the list goes on. Every day I was evolving, and everything around me was changing fast. During this time, Tupac and Biggie would be murdered, and my life would mimic the art I loved. The entire time change was happening, I knew I just had to escape and follow my college dream. It didn't matter that, on a daily basis, I heard I wasn't smart enough or good enough for college. My heart always told me I could. My advice to you is never let anyone talk you out of your dreams. As long as you believe them, follow them with all of your heart and soul.

Walk in Love

When your day goes bad here is what you do
Open your bible and learn about what is true
Jesus teaches us to love all
That doesn't mean you won't get disrespected or suddenly fall
Some will judge you when you hurt them
Please know one thing you're more precious than
any precious gem
Every day you live is an opportunity to serve God
No need to own weapons or even to carry a heavy rod
The more you forgive the longer you will live
It's not about possessions, it's all about how much you give
Give thanks to our God who sits high above
We shall be humbled and consistently walk in love

CHAPTER 2

DEATH AROUND THE CORNER

With only a few years left of high school, my focus began to shift to college. Unfortunately, my friends stayed the same, and trouble was always right around the corner. My mother had dreams of seeing me stay close to home for college, but that was not an option for me. I had to get out of Connecticut fast. I knew staying in Connecticut would probably lead to my death. Most of my friends at this time had issues with the law, and the majority of my childhood friends were not even graduating high school. Death would show up and remind me that it was right at my doorstep.

After leaving the basketball court, I would go to see my best friend at work. He worked at a local grocery store down the street from the park. We would laugh and joke as he was stocking the shelves. One night we had planned to go to a party near a lake. As I left his job, something didn't feel right. I still remember to this day leaving his job and feeling unsettled. Like most teenagers, we had a pre-party, and so I went to my friend Jason's house. We smoked weed and drank before leaving for the main party. Back then we didn't have cell phones; we had land lines and pagers. The plan was to meet my best friend at the lake party around 10 p.m. At 9 p.m., I was already high and intoxicated, so I decided to take a little nap.

I would get a call a 3 am at Jason's, only to learn my best friend had drowned in the lake. I thought it was a joke until the news spread throughout the town and everyone began calling. I was supposed to be with him. Leaving his job that night was the last time I would see him alive. How had I overslept? Why had I not been there? I thought that if I had been there, he would not have died.

My heart was shattered, and the funeral was so hard to go to. How could I look his family in the face? I felt completely responsible for his death. I knew he couldn't swim, but did the others know that? Months would go by, and still healing did not take place. Going to his funeral caused me so much pain because I finally realized that I was not untouchable.

More time passed, and I would go on to lose another best friend. He was stabbed to death at a party. He would die in the back seat of my other friend's car, bleeding to death before they could reach the hospital. Another party I was supposed to be at. You see, all these places where I was supposed to be, and all these tragic outcomes. My mind kept telling me, *You're next. You're next.* I listened to these voices and felt like death was right around the corner.

On top of these deaths, some of my close friends were heading off to jail because of drug sales. The walls were closing in on me, and I knew I had to get out fast. All of these outcomes were right near me.

⁂

The highlight of my basketball career was making the Junior National Team for Connecticut. I would go on to represent Connecticut basketball in the Junior Olympics. Out of two hundred kids, they picked twelve. I played my best basketball during tryouts, but most of my family members told me not to get my hopes up. The minute I left, though, I knew I'd made that team.

One of my best friends, Kirk, drove me down to Central State Connecticut University to cheer me on. When we got back, he told everyone I'd made the team before we even knew for sure. I went to the mailbox every day for a month checking to see. There was no letter, and I began to feel doubtful. Everyone kept telling me the odds were against me. Then one day the letter came! I was among the twelve guys who'd made the team, and I would have the opportunity to go to Columbus, Ohio to compete.

When we went out to Columbus, it was one big party. You had hundreds of kids in one hotel with no parental supervision. Every night we partied, and I met a lot of girls from all over the country. Unfortunately, I would not take advantage of the biggest opportunity presented to me because I was consumed in partying with girls and drugs while attending the Junior Nationals competition. That year in Columbus, Ohio, I would end up walking away from basketball after a new, inexperienced coach was hired. Our team was in last place, and I knew my focus had to be on running. One of my biggest regrets was quitting the team before the season ended, but I knew it was the right thing for me to do. I shifted my energy into running track and started my season early. Many people were shocked that I'd walked away from the game I loved—so was I—but I knew I had to get out. I would go on to win conference and class "SS" states and position myself as a legitimate Division 1 athlete.

While all of this was going on, my grandfather came to live with us. He had been diagnosed with lung cancer, and it began to spread rapidly throughout his lungs. At this time, my grandmother could not take care of my grandfather, so my mother volunteered to help. Watching my grandfather die right in front of me every day was painful. I remember when the nurse told my grandpa was going to die, and that he had accepted it. The man had more courage than any man I would ever know. He went on hospice and died shortly after.

The night he died, I saw what I thought were people walking into his room, but the next day, my mother told me no one had entered his room. After speaking to my grandma, she convinced me that those were angels bringing him home. From that day forward, I was obsessed with angels.

With my grandfather gone, I refocused on the mission to go to college. I spent hours reaching out to universities, but the minute I sent out my high school transcripts, the communication would go dark. I had no clue how much grades mattered. I had been told I could go wherever I wanted to go, but that was not accurate one bit due to my GPA. The dream of going to college was beginning to look dim and unrealistic.

I continued to think positive and carry on in my pursuit to achieve a college degree, but this was a dark period in my life because I would learn lot about death. I would learn it didn't care about age, race, or status. The pain I held was at the highest point, and my future looked dim.

You Just Never Know

Before bed I pray to the Lord
Will my message be received, or do I need a cord?
I see happiness and joy in our future
Serving, loving, and even a teacher
You mean so much to me
Just the thought of us all together brings me glee
Imagine us all going around the world
Maybe diving under water and seeking beautiful white pearls
Or what about a trip to the moon
How about a sunny hot day in a hot air balloon?
A cruise to the freezing North Pole
I think on a Caribbean island fishing with a long narrow pole
All of us in Paris on top of the Eiffel tower
The thought of standing in the rain playing near
thousands of colorful flowers
You can have anything in this life if you're willing to grow
Close your eyes and imagine, you just never know

CHAPTER 3

VIRGINIA

I was scared. My time in high school was running out, and my options were going away. My principal at the time would have an encounter with me, which would motivate me to do the impossible. At this age, I was at times very immature, and I loved to pick on my principal. I would see him in the hall, and showing off for my friends, I'd scream his name out loud and be rude. Back then, you never called an adult by their first name.

He came up to me, grab me by my arm, would look into my eyes, and say, "Call me by my first name when you get a college degree!"

I was shocked and upset. I took it as him saying I would never attain such a gift. This was much-needed motivation to prove him wrong and everyone else who thought I wasn't smart enough.

Every day after that, my life consisted of filling out college applications and praying that a university would give me a shot. I had applied at Norfolk State University, an historical black college in Norfolk, Virginia, because my brother lived near the area. I contacted their basket-ball coach and told him about making Junior Nationals. The interest was there, and I would be accepted to attend the university. Finally, I had an opening and a bridge out of Connecticut.

At this point, running was not even in my thoughts. Basketball was resurrected, and when I attended the fresh-man walk-through, I met with the coach and finalized our conversation. But the minute school started, I searched for the basketball coach only to find out he had just been fired! I was in complete shock. Once again, my back was up against the wall. I could only attend classes and wait for tryouts to happen.

As I was in class one day, I was called out to the hall-way because my financial aid did not cover all my costs. I was told I had to come up with two thousand dollars or forfeit my education. I called everyone in my immedi-ate family, and no one could help me. I cried at the pay phone, with my calling card minutes running out. I made one last call to my Aunt Phyllis and begged her to loan me the money. Thank God she wired the money, and I was good for a semester. Later on in the week, I would contact my mother and have her send me all of my articles and clippings from high school. I was preparing to make my case to the track and cross-country coach.

After receiving all my newspaper articles and awards, I headed to the track office to meet the coaches. I literally popped in off the street and made my case. The coach was impressed by my high school achievements and gave me an opportunity to walk on the team. He assured me that if

I came to practice and kept my grades up, next semester he would cover my expenses. I agreed, and another door had opened up.

When I showed up to practice, most of the guys were from other countries. We would meet at 6am and travel to a local park to run. The running started off easy, and then the pace would become intense. I would then find out we had another practice at 3 p.m. to work on speed. Yes, that's right: practice was two times a day, and you had to stay up on your studies. When people say that colligate athletes have it easy, it tells me one thing: They were never a colligate athlete. In addition to traveling Wednesday through Sunday, and the extreme practice hours, and oh, by the way, the pressure to compete at a high level in order to keep your scholarship, there was the navigation of constant distractions—the parties and the girls. Life had just hit me so hard in the face that I was rocked by the expectations. All of my life I had been chasing this dream even when people told me I couldn't do this—that I wasn't smart enough, that I wasn't fast enough, that I wasn't at the right high school, and on and on. The attitude I had was simple. I was on a mission. What waited for me back in Connecticut was defeat, pain, and my past. I had to prove everyone wrong, and I had to prove myself right.

Going into my freshman year of competing, I was fighting to make the team. Let me say that again—I was fighting just to make the team. Most of the runners were elite African runners. But before I could compete with them, I had to compete with a local phenom. He was all-state in Virginia and a hometown hero. I could care less who he was, but I would study his every move. In practice, I would show him I was crazy, without fear. He was on a full scholarship, and all that meant to me was that he was holding onto my opportunity. I questioned the workouts and even questioned the coaching a lot. Also, we were sponsored by Asics, and our shoes felt like concrete bricks, but we would go on to win conference with me as the seventh man on the starting line-up.

I was the seventh runner on the team, barely making the roster. I wasn't settling for being the seventh man, so I started to strategize. How could I get to the next level and compete with the African guys on the team? How could I get an edge?

I spoke with a guy from my high school who went to school with my older brother. He was an excellent colligate runner who ate, slept, and lived running. He lived in Surprise, Arizona, which was in the middle of nowhere. We decided that me going out there would help him train, and help me train, but he warned me it would not be fun.

When I got out there, I found that he didn't have a TV, and his wife was pretty religious. We spent thirty days running two times a day and learning how to run strong. We would wake up at 5am and run intervals, then run for twenty minutes in the pool. In Arizona, the temperature sometimes hit 90 degrees by 7 a.m. It was hot and uncomfortable.

After our morning routine, I would rest and wake up at noon to lift weights and ride my bike a few miles, then wait for him to get home from work and do an intense night workout on the canals. Canals were all dirt with no light. It was like running with my eyes closed. I would learn how to conquer fear and my emotions through running on the canals. You would hear snakes and scorpions gliding through the dirt. We also would attend a high attitude camp at Northern Arizona University to get in some high-altitude training.

Going to Arizona really taught me how to run. I learned the mental dynamic of running and how to take care of my body. When I returned from Arizona, I was running so fast everyone thought I was on enhancement drugs. I went from barely making the team to competing with our top three runners. I knew I was getting fast when I walked off the track, and a man from the NCAA followed me to the bathroom and told me to pee into a cup. It was crazy, but I was glad to see them keeping the sport clean. Competitive drugs were available to athletes, and a lot of athletes took them. The pressure was so high that some felt the need to have that edge.

I was a blue-collar runner and loved working hard, day in and day out. There was nothing fancy about me. I wanted to break my competition through hard work. My greatest accomplishments in college were being a 3x cross-country all-conference, finishing second in the 5k and second in the steeple chase, scoring 18 points in our MEAC Championship. Our team track and cross-country teams won MEAC conference six times and many other collegiate meet accomplishments.

During my career as a runner, I also would have on-campus jobs working in the cafeteria, mail room, and in the computer lab. My face became very recognizable because I was everywhere around campus. I worked hard to acquire my college degree.

Eventually, I would move off campus into a two-bedroom apartment with five other guys. We had roaches and water bugs, and sometimes our living conditions were horrible. We were right off campus but dead smack in the ghetto. Gunshots and drug users were common-place. Fortunately, I became friends with all the local drug dealers and stick-up kids, so I was never harmed. I spoke to everyone in the neighborhood and got close to them all. Many nights it saved me from getting robbed because they all knew me.

Mission College was the name of our low-income housing neighborhood, and to this day it is not a safe place to be. My brother would come pick me up and see kids riding their bikes at midnight. He asked what I was doing living over there. I told him I had no choice because it was the only thing I could afford.

As college life went on, the group of guys I was hanging with would evolve into a tight group. Most people today ask how I got involved with being in a fraternity because I was not pro fraternity when I got down to school. One of my best friends got picked on for wearing this greek jacket—Phi Delta Psi. Arrens or aka Ace was my friend from freshman orientation, and I had his back. At the time, I couldn't stand fraternities because they just seemed loud and annoying. They got on my nerves with their stepping and dancing. One day, I'd had enough of seeing Ace get picked on and decided to research his fraternity.

"All that we put into the lives of others comes back into our own."

I read that and was hooked. Phi Delta Psi fraternity was all about uplifting the community and helping those in need. I had a vision of helping an unknown fraternity on campus become a big-name fraternity. That's who I was—someone who went against the grain. I could have joined a well-known fraternity, but why not create a new legacy? The brothers in that fraternity are still my brothers to this day. We would grow the fraternity to fifteen members and be one of the most popular fraternities on campus when I attended school at Norfolk State. In addition to that, we helped our local community by hosting Easter egg hunts, helped out at food drives, and helped out at assisted living communities. In my opinion, that is what fraternities should be about and these group of men will always remain my brothers for life.

CHAPTER 4

ROSSLYN STATION

"When you loved someone and had to let them go, there will always be that small part of yourself that whispers, what was it that you wanted and why didn't you fight for it."—Source Shannon L Alder

While attending school at Norfolk State University I would visit my brother and his wife from time to time because they lived right outside of Washington DC. They had a large house and lived in a beautiful neighborhood. My niece and nephew were really young and I enjoyed spending time with them as well too. It was a nice break from the unsettling inner city life that Norfolk provided.

For the first time in my life, I would experience this thing called love. While visiting my brother I decided to go into DC to party at a well-known club. It was three floors and each floor had its own gene of music. I was feeling good and looking good and even met Montel Jordan that night accidently. He was so tall but very nice guy. At the time, he had a great music hit out called "this how we do it." After meeting him I decided to go upstairs to another level of the club and look around more. The energy was high, and the people were having a blast.

The club was jam packed, and one of my favorite songs came on. I decided to dance to the song, and I saw a gorgeous woman to dance with. She was German and African-American (I would later find out), and I couldn't take my eyes off her. When the song ended, I asked her for her number, and she said no.

Now at this point in my life I was very charming and arrogant, so hearing no through me off. She told me if it was meant to be, I would see her again. Well there were hundreds of people in this club, so the odds were not with me.

After she left me, I spent the entire night looking for her. It was if she just vanished in thin air. No other woman in the entire club stood out to me because she was trapped in my head. I ended up telling my friend that I came with about her and he told me you will never see her again. I was so determined that I went to every single floor and searched long and hard for her whereabouts. Finally, I realized that the possibility of me finding her was not realistic. The feeling that I had was new because I never felt this feeling before. It was different and strange.

Suddenly the lights would come on and the music would stop. I looked up and there she was. I gently grab her hand and she smiled. I told her, "see it was meant to be!" She smiled and gave me her number. I remember driving home thinking of the amazing feeling. Her smile was so captivating and electric.

Out of respect for her I won't say her name, but we would go on to talk and email all the time. We went on multiple dates and she would even introduce me to grape leaves. I think that was the last time I ate those. I would travel up to DC to see her and my stop was Rosslyn station. Her smile was so beautiful and her teeth so white. She was intellectual—going school to get her degree. The world stop every time I saw her.

The distance made our relationship hard and eventually I knew I would be leaving Virginia. Deep down inside I loved her and knew I would make a big mistake not trying harder. She was everything I wanted in a woman. Ironically, I have never had that feeling again. Every now and again I reach out to her, but I know I broke her heart.

When you find true love protect it and embrace it because you never know if you will ever see it again. It has been twenty years and I never felt that way again. If I could just rewind the hands on the clock but I can't.

It was important for me to share that story with you because we have doubted love. I know I did in that moment. What would life be like if I embraced the moment. Every now and then I go on social media and see her picture and wonder. Time doesn't wait up or stand still for any of us. The experience will forever be on my soul.

GRATEFUL FOR BLESSINGS

All that we get comes from our Lord
No weapon can hurt us not even a sword
Some will love you while others will hate
God will judge your heart when you get to the His gate
Our time must be spent in the right kind of way
Don't worry the weather even if its gloomy and grey
Salvation and compassion will set you free
The words are in the holy bible they came with a fee
This blessing was sent from the holy spirit
Be strong and courageous while you become rich
Our past does not define who we truly are
Yes, we will have proof with an unforeseen scar
Learn this gospel as if it was a lesson
Always be grateful for Blessings

CHAPTER 5

IT'S YOUR FATHER

As my colligate career blossomed and the recognition grew, I wondered what my father was up to. Some days I would imagine calling him up and telling him how far I had come. For some reason, I was never upset with him for being absent.

It was the end of my sophomore year at school, and my friend from Arizona called me and asked if I wanted to participate in a race back home. I had no expectations of winning the race, and I didn't even know who would be in it. I told him, sure, why not. I was in fantastic shape, and my game plan was to run a fast first mile. At the time, I was working on my mile time, so this would be a perfect training.

When I got to the race, he had a high school jersey in his car, so I asked if I could wear that. Stafford was on the jersey, and I felt honored to represent my hometown. I also saw some of the reporters from back when I ran in high school, so I got a little bit nervous, and excited.

We got to the start line, and the gun went off. I ran so fast from the gun I felt like I was floating in the air. My first mile was like 4:30, and I still had a few miles to go. I felt great until the last mile but ran all alone. At the end of the race, my friend began to creep up behind me, but by that time, the race was over. I won. They would put me on the back page of the *Journal Inquirer*: "Uphill battle goes to Hightower!" I was happy to see that I took up the back page of the paper, and everyone from my town was talking about it. I was so humble because I had no intention of winning the race an was simply honored to wear an old high school jersey again. Most athletes are competitive and want to win every race this is true however I utilized this race as a training exercise.

Later on in the week, I received a phone call that would rock my world. My father reached out to me and asked me to meet him at a restaurant in Hartford. I was happy and a little confused. The last time I saw my father, I was in middle school, and I remember he took me to the mall to get a few clothes. After that, he went dark for almost ten years.

My father found me because of the article in the newspaper. When I met him, I was blown away by how much I looked like him. My father was bald, handsome, and talked to everyone in the restaurant. I was so happy to sit down and have a conversation. He smiled a lot and promised to keep in touch.

I would later find out his nickname was kojack because he looked like the star of the old television series. He had a steady job, and I was told that he even bootlegged alcohol on the weekends. He had a long, brown Cadillac, and everyone knew him in the north end of Hartford.

That would be the last time I ever saw my father. We would go on to have a few phone conversations, but that would be the last time we ever met. What made the dynamic difficult was that my father had his own family, and his relationship with my mother had not been a committed situation—it had been an affair. I knew my mother loved him deeply because she would always tell me she did. Even though she would go on to marry my stepdad, in her heart my father was her soulmate.

Not having my father around really did affect me in a large way. At times it hurt my confidence and left a void in my heart and soul. I would spend my entire adolescent life searching for a man to follow. Sometimes I sit and wonder what would life would have been like with a father. Would I be stronger or weaker? My father said a lot of things to me, and they all sounded good, but the reality of his words never came true. Being mad at him never simplified the problem or made things better, so I never invested in that energy. I just wanted to show him that I'd made it and to have him in my life.

The greatest gift my father gave me was the gift to be a great father. I tell that to people, and they look at me like I am crazy. Without the pain and the mistrust that he gave me, I could never love my daughters the way I do. My daughters will never feel the pain I once felt as a child. He gave me the gift of fatherhood by being absent. It was a true blessing because I know what the other side feels like. As a parent, how could you make a baby and go absent? I will never know because my daughters will never feel such a pain in their hearts. I never knew what led my father to these actions, so how could I judge him? In life, we know half of a story and seem to judge others. Not me, because I grew up with people prejudging me constantly. How my father grew up, and what he was exposed to in his life, I just don't know. The moral of the story is this: I forgive him. He paid his child support, and he did his best in life. Unfortunately, he missed out on me, and at the end of the day, that's okay. When we hold on to negative energy, how will that help us grow? It will not help us grow, so the alternative is to forgive and move on.

WE KNOW NOTHING

In the twilight of our being;
We know nothing
In the womb of our existence;
We know nothing
In the annuals of our mind;
We know nothing
In the fabric of our life;
We know nothing
In our forced labor;
We know nothing
In our delivery;
We know nothing
In our execution;
We know nothing
In our untimely death;
We know nothing
But in Jesus Christ;
We know everything!
Signed... Confessions of the forgotten fetus.

Cynthia K. Lee

CHAPTER 6

BROKEN RELATIONSHIPS

While at the mall one day, I was approached by an employee of a jewelry store to sell jewelry during the summers and off seasons. The employee was an elegant lady named Mrs. Tami. She somehow convinced me to fill out a job application to sell jewelry at the store where she worked. I thought selling jewelry was absurd, but when I found out how much I could make I was all in. All I had to do was dress nice and be around the beautiful women who worked there.

Selling jewelry would bring out a skill in me I never knew I had—effective communication. You see, to convince someone to buy something they don't necessarily need is a great gift. It is the art of persuasion.

I would see all my friends, as the mall was the place to be on the weekends. I loved working jewelry and loved the women who would constantly come in to browse. I also learned a lot about myself. It felt good to look nice and professional. Also, the rush I got from selling a diamond ring was like nothing I'd ever felt. I would see couples who had been married for over forty years, and I became fascinated by true love.

Selling jewelry also introduced me to the woman I would marry. I knew the minute I saw her I would marry her. Instantly, I knew. I guess you could say it was love at first sight. It wouldn't be easy, though, because I had developed a reputation around the mall as a player—meaning I dated a lot of women who worked within the mall. I sent notes to her daily and had the guys at the store where she worked act as messengers. It didn't matter that she was in a relationship, and I was not her type.

After a year, she finally caved in and went on a date with me to the Norfolk Zoo. If you ask her, she will tell you it wasn't a real date. She let me know that she had never been to a zoo, so it was a friendly gathering. Nonetheless, I will call it a date because it took me a year to hang out with her. Eventually the hard work to court her paid off. We became a couple and eventually married. Our marriage lasted almost ten years, and after multiple affairs and lies, she served me with divorce papers. Although we saw the world, bought fancy cars, lived in beautiful homes, and traveled to exotic places, happiness just couldn't come in to the relationship. I was lost and out of control because of money and power. She had every right to eventually leave me, and I was surprised she didn't do it sooner.

I don't want to spend a lot of time discussing my ex because, in all reality, the cut has not yet healed. I am grateful for the thirteen years she spent with me, and I am blessed to have had two beautiful daughters with her. At the end of a marriage, everyone wants to be right and everyone wants to blame the other person. Let me say this: I made mistakes, but I did my best. The folks on her side will go on to believe I am a monster, a villain, and that's okay because everyone is entitled to their own opinion. Here is what I know for a fact, though. I am a great father to my daughters, and I failed miserably as a husband. I own that fact, and life goes on. After all, in life we are all going to fail, and those who judge me should look at their own lives. How could I love any woman in my life when I had this void, the pain from my father and the on and off relationship with my mother? I would try to destroy relationships because I knew eventually they would destroy themselves.

Today, my ex-wife has moved on, and so have I. We were young, and I had no business getting married to her. Since our pain is still fresh and real, I will put aside our differences and wish her well.

RELATIONSHIPS THAT MATTER

People will come, and people will go
Some provide laughter others will help you to grow
Others will leave a never-ending mark on your soul
A few may leave you in questioning creating a hole
God will enlighten you with those that cross your path
If you can calculate this becomes simple math
Nothing just happens for no reason
Yes, there is a higher power, He will provide several seasons
Be careful of the words you speak and how you talk
Your reality becomes real in which how you walk
Doesn't matter how tall or short your stature
Will you ultimately be on the right side before the rapture
Eat abundantly from God's gracious platter
We all have meaning so does the relationships that matter

CHAPTER 7

AN OLYMPIAN IS BORN

During my time at Norfolk State, I encountered and befriended one of the best runners with whom I have ever had the privilege to run. He was a red shirt freshman, a high school All-American, and an adopted kid from Sudan who went to high school in upstate New York. His adopted family was from upstate New York, and he entered into high school after leaving a Kenyan refugee camp.

As the captain of the team, it was my job to take the new guy under my wing and make sure he was okay. The first workout we did was an eight-mile pace run, and we were running six-minute intervals. When we came through the mile markers, he knew exactly what the pace was without a watch, and he impressed me significantly. I told my coach I have never seen anything like this from a freshman. College, Division 1 is an entirely different ball game from high school. It's almost impossible to be a Division 1 athlete—you have to be incredibly good.

Lopez Lomong escaped a Sudan war, and escaped after being kidnapped as a kid by Kenyan police. He stayed in a refugee camp for years. God would show up for him. When he told me his story, I got chills, and I knew that he and I meeting was God's calling. Our friendship flourished, and he expressed to me his dream of going to the Olympics.

He was running a low, four-minute mile right out of high school, and he was not far away from Olympic qualifiers. At the time, I had a great relationship with some of the coaches from Arizona, and their team was nationally ranked. I brought up Lopez in a conversation while in Arizona, and the rest is history. As I was leaving Norfolk to pursue my career in Arizona, Lopez and I had a vision of him running in Arizona for the top-ranked school. I may have upset some people in helping him out with this process, but he knew where he wanted to go, and I did what any good friend would do. He would go on to win NCAA and become an All-American by his sophomore year of college. I watched him win his title, and I knew this would be the beginning of something special.

Lopez was the true meaning of the American dream. After breaking all his university's records, he would go pro and sign with Nike. He participated in multiple Olympics and broke American records while doing so. Lopez gave me the greatest gift of all time. I received a call one day, and he asked me if my daughters could be the flower girls in his wedding. This gesture touched my soul, and I was honored by this gift. Our paths had not crossed by accident. God was present, in my opinion.

Through my college career, I had hundreds of relationships with people, and I wish I could put every relationship in this book. But this relationship had to be told and had to be talked about. When we question faith, and when we question God, I always think of Lopez. To be kidnapped as a kid and escape death, then to go on to be a world-wide athlete on the biggest stage? That's not luck. That isn't anything other than faith. People come in and out of our lives for a reason, and Lopez coming into my life was instrumental to showing me in life anything is possible when we put our faith in God. Hearing his story on how far he came told me one thing, God has to be real! During my darkest days, I always thought about Lopez and what he endured escaping from Sudanese rebels as a child. When you follow Jesus, this is proof that anything is possible.

1983. Alex, Tommy, Chrissy.

Grandpa and Grandma Sgarellino.

Norfolk State Graduation Tom Hightower,
first person from my family to get a four-year degree.

1991. Tommy, Alex, Chrissy, and Jennifer.

My beautiful mother as a baby.

Executive Tom Hightower at YP.com.
(Billion Dollar Media company)

1995. Tommy, Angela, Morgan, Alex, Marlon, Kiana, Chrissy, and Jennifer.

*2008. Lopez Lomong, Tommy, and my oldest daughter
Gianna right after the Olympics. Lopez came to visit
us after the Olympic games.*

Phi Delta Psi fraternity and the Sapphires, my brothers and sisters for life. Mike Temple, Donte Lucas, RIP Thaddeus James, Norman Forrest, Dwanye Kindrick, Trav Rutlege, Arrens Cange, Grant, Jeff Easely, Jay, Dr. Joey Rosario, Jeff Lewis, Big Mark, and Carlton Winston. Kappa Chapter, Norfolk State.

My mother with Gianna and Ava in Florence, Italy.

2016. Gianna and Ava Hightower. Rome, Italy.

*Grandma and Grandpa with my mother and
auntie Phyllis in their younger years.*

ONE Commitment... TEAMWORK

Spartan freshman Juan Serrano had a memorable season on the baseball team. A first-team All-MEAC infielder, Serrano became the first-ever NSU player named MEAC Rookie of the Year. He also set a new school record by getting a hit in nine consecutive at-bats, and was named a Louisville Slugger Freshman All-American.

Men's basketball player Chakawby Hicks and baseball player Darryl Chever made the All-MEAC first team in their respective sports, and finished in the top 10 nationally in a statistical category. Hicks finished third in the nation with 3.0 steals per game, and Chever finished fourth with 0.2 triples per game.

Women's basketball coach James Sweat joined select company by winning his 500th career game on Feb. 9 at South Carolina State. He was later presented with the game ball, signed by his players and assistant coaches, to commemorate the event.

The NSU Athletics Foundation presented the athletics department with $50,000 in proceeds from the foundation's first annual scholarship car raffle. Wendell Bates of Chesapeake won the grand prize, a 2003 Kia Sorento SUV, donated by the Southern Hospitality Automotive Group.

Eight worthy former Spartan athletes, coaches and supporters were inducted into the NSU Athletics Foundation Sports Hall of Fame in August 2003. The inductees were: LaRue Harrington, a football player from 1976-79; Tracy Saunders, a women's basketball player from 1987-91; Rudy Peele, a men's basketball player from 1968-72; Chandra Sturrup, a women's track athlete from 1992-95; Marty Miller, a baseball player from 1965-68; Charles Christian, the men's basketball coach from 1974-78 and 1982-90; William 'Dick' Price, former head football and track coach and athletics director;

and Rosa Alexander, an avid Spartan football and band supporter who donated much of her time and money to NSU and its athletics department.

Spartan men's athletic programs finished second in the 2003-04 MEAC all-sports standings. NSU tallied 54 points, second only to Hampton's 55.5. The NSU women finished in seventh place with 43 points.

For their accomplishments, Kevin Talley and Tianna Golding were named NSU Male and Female Athlete of the Year, respectively. Men's tennis player Jakub Novak was named NSU's Scholar Athlete of the Year with a 3.91 GPA in business management. He was also named to the MEAC Commissioner's All-Academic Team and the second-team All-MEAC in singles for the Spartans.

Norfolk State University news article highlighting our conference championship. Achieved All-Conference.

February 19, 2017. My baptism at Smoky Hill Vineyard Church. The day I gave my life to Christ.

Cynthia Lee, my guardian angel. Thank you for your spiritual guidance, love, and visionary mind.

1999. High School Graduation from Stafford High.
Alex, Kiana, Jennifer, and Chrissy.

Ant Attalla, Isaac Cruz, Ed Grant, Brandon Prescott,
and Sharif Dyson in Las Vegas.

RIP Big Phil and Maureen Balanceau.

Tom Hightower breezes toward the finish line ahead of Clint Santoro at the Summer Grand Prix Series at Wickham Park on Monday.

Uphill battle goes to Hightower

By Matt Buckler
Journal Inquirer

MANCHESTER — Yes Virginia, there are some hills at Wickham Park. Tough ones, as a matter of fact.

Climbing those hills at high speed was the only adjustment Thomas Hightower of Stafford needed to make as he stomped to a win in the opening race of the Summer Grand Prix Cross Country Race Series here Monday. His time was 13:58 on the hot, humid night.

"There are no hills in Virginia," said Hightower, 22, who is preparing for his junior year at Norfolk State University. "I'm used to the flat courses they have there. This course is deadly to me."

You'd never know it by the way he controlled the start of the race. Hightower opened up a huge lead — by the time he blasted his way into the East Hartford end of Wickham Park, everyone else was still in Manchester.

"That was the strategy," Hightower said. "I just went out hard and got going."

It worked. Clint Santoro, a fellow Stafford High graduate, passed Nick AuYeung of Manchester at the end of the race to take second. But he was nine seconds behind Hightower.

"My time was horrendous, probably my worst since my sophomore year in high school," Santoro, 27, said. "I don't think I had any business even finishing second."

Hightower's winning margin was deceiving. After carving open a huge lead, he slanted into cruise control during the second half of the race.

"I had no one to run with, so after the mile, I shut it down," Hightower said. "It felt like I was just jogging at the end."

Hightower, who plans to specialize in the 3,000-meter steeplechase next year in college, decided to start his summer running season early this year.

"Last year I only took four weeks off after track season, but this year I only took two months off after track season. And I got right back into training," Hightower said. "And now I'm headed to Arizona to train with Clint for a month. I really should be ready for the cross country season."

Even if they sneak in a course with hills in it.

The defending champion, meanwhile, was off to a fast start in the female division. Heather Gardiner toured the 2.6-mile course in 15:08 to finish first in the female class. She finished 18th overall.

"I was pretty happy, I guess," Gardiner said. "I try to race every race hard, because I love to compete. But because I race so often, I can't take them all that seriously. If I did, I think I would burn myself out."

Gardiner, 23, a graduate of Central Connecticut State University, says she races at least once a week. The key race for her this summer will be an eight-miler in Stowe, Vt., on July 21.

"But the long-range goal is the Hartford Marathon later this year," Gardiner said, "but that isn't in October."

Bo doubt she'll have a lot of races under her belt between now and then. Joanna Higgins of Tolland was second behind Gardiner, clocked in 17:13.

Levi DeValve won the one-mile youth race in 6:10 followed by Seth DeValve in 6:44 and Cameron Ware in 6:49. Kaitlin Bellamy was the first female finisher in 7:05.

Race No. 2 in the summer series, sponsored by the Journal Inquirer, the Silk City Striders, Wickham Park and Outback Steakhouse, will take place on Monday, July 22, with the youth race at 6 p.m. and the adult race at 6:30 p.m.

Adult Race

1. Thomas Hightower, 13:36; 2. Clint Santoro, 13:47; 3. Nick Au Yeung, 13:54; 4. David Metzger, 13:54; 5. Jon Busch, 13:59; 6. Matt Dilibo, 14:07; 7. Justin Jablonowski, 14:12; 8. Mike LeMay, 14:19; 9. Paul Gaffari, 14:29; 10. Colin Carroll, 14:30.
11. Mike Tortora, 14:33; 12. Jerild Kid, 14:42; 13. Jeffrey Stenzel, 14:42; 14. Pete Chudzik, 14:46; 15. Mike McCall, 14:45; 16. Mike Munroe, 14:55; 17. Steven Morse, 15:01; 18. Heather Gardiner, 15:06; 19. Lance Flamino, 15:14; Matt Conyers, 15:15.
21. Kevin Glenn, 15:19; 22. Joe Kidder, 15:19; 23. Matt Mills, 15:29; 24. Neal Leibowitz, 15:47; 25. Tim Blinn, 15:54; 26. Jeff Lukach, 15:57; 27. Doug Flamino, 15:59; 28. Jay Seney, 16:05; 29. Bill Metzger, 16:13; 30. Jeff Keepper, 16:22.
31. Steve McLaughlin, 16:29; 32. Ken Erikson, 16:37; 33. Rich White, 16:42; 34. Tyler Burnell, 16:43; 35. Bruce Eanneker, 16:44; 36. Tony Hollister, 16:45; 37. Tris Carta, 16:52; 38. David Taylor, 16:53; 39. Peter Briggeman, 16:57; 40. Joanna Higgins, 17:13.
41. Mark Powers, 17:15; 42. Tom Butterfield; 43. Dan Pendergraph, 17:28; 44. Roy Frost, 17:30; 46. James Pingree, 17:46; 47. Pat Byrne, 18:08; 48. Bekki Wright, 18:09; 49. Toby Schoeneberger, 18:10; 50. Rich Connors, 18:16.
51. Kristin Metzger, 18:31; 53. Jerry Levasseur, 18:35; 54. Clint Driscoll, 18:41; 55. Tyler Carrigan, 18:57; 56. Kristen Gonc, 19:11; 57. Theresa Bombrowski, 19:16; 58. Ryan Powers, 19:19; 60. Michael Leska, 19:26.
61. Sam Pendergraph, 19:26; 62. Allie Lemire, 19:28; 63. Randall Potterton, 19:30; 64. Dani Kennedy, 19:32; 67. Sherry Wallace, 19:59; 68. Joan McGuire, 20:07; 69. Joe Quinn, 20:32; 70. Daniel Usher, 20:35.
70. Daaisi Usher, 20:35; 71. Elizabeth Oblon, 20:38; 72. Thomas Baliotto, 20:43; 73. Sue Leslie, 20:43; 74. Erin Leska, 21:02; 75. Kevin Basis, 21:26; 76. AJ Doerr, 21:40; 77. Lisa Yagnloff, 21:40; 78. Jacki Marchitto, 22:00; 79. Stefanie Keepper, 22:02; 80. Chip Ware, 22:05.
81. Mary Lou White, 22:31; 82. Betty Cannella, 22:37; 83. Chad Rosenberg, 23:17; 84. Joe Zimmerman, 23:31; 85. Barbara Dell, 23:34; 86. Diane Snow, 22:34; 87. Kathy Thornton, 23:42; 88. Janit Romayko, 22:46; 89. Laura DeValve, 33:58; 90. James Hodgen, 25:04; 91. Peg Symonds, 25:15.

"Uphill Battle goes to Hightower"

Gianna's Preschool Graduation.
Gianna on the left, and Ava on the right.

A Miracle from Heaven

When we pray can God really hear us
Life gets so hard how do we trust
Lately I hear Jesus saying a lot
At times when I pray I get really overwhelmed and hot
Some say that is the Holy Spirit sharing the love
Others would argue that this is Gods touch from above
Continue to pray and allow God in your heart
Don't worry about the ending just create a wonderful start
Remember one thing Jesus doesn't owe us a thing
Not a house, not a car, or even a ring.
He died for all of our sins
At the end of the game it really doesn't matter who loses or wins
We live on this earth to serve each other
Also loving our brother, sister, father, and mother
Age means nothing even if your younger then eleven
I pray that God unites our family gives us a
miracle from Heaven

CHAPTER 8

THE IMPOSSIBLE

Graduation day was near, and I already had plans to leave Virginia. This was the moment I'd been waiting for since I was twelve years old and hanging college posters on my walls. Everyone would be present except my aunt. She wasn't big on traveling, so she stayed at home. The absence of my aunt hurt inside. She was the one on the other end of the phone when I was in desperate need. Her loan to me kept me on my journey. I will forever be in debt to her for that deed. Fortunately, I paid her back in full immediately after graduating college.

The ceremony was surreal and fast, so it seemed. I don't remember much of my graduation because I was in awe that it was even happening. All the teachers, guidance counselors, critics, friends, family members, enemies, and haters would all be proven wrong in this moment. All those who said I couldn't acquire a four-year degree from a university were wrong. All those who said I couldn't go Division 1 in athletics were wrong. Did I get joy from proving everyone wrong? Yes, I did. Was it easy? Was it simple? No, it was not. The greatest accomplishment I ever achieved was graduating school and running Division 1. I knew that I'd set the standard for the kids I would eventually have.

I hear people say all the time that college isn't important. College isn't about a degree. College is about setting a goal and executing on that goal. Graduating represents adversity, pain, obstacles, love, defeat, and winning. My university made me a man, and I will forever be grateful for that opportunity.

After the graduation ceremony, we went to my exwife's mother's house to celebrate my accomplishment. It would be the last time both sides of our families would unite for a gathering. My ex and I decided that I would go out to Arizona first by myself to get settle. Two days after my graduation, I took my '91 Nissan Sentra cross-country to Phoenix, Arizona. My aunt worked for a national mortgage lender, and they were hiring in Phoenix. They offered a college graduate program for hungry college grads, and then they transferred you to a territory when training is complete.

The drive to Arizona took me three days, and it was scary at times. While making the drive out there I didn't think too much of my girlfriend and probably should have ended it in Virginia. I had all my belongings in the car, so I couldn't even see out the back window. I stopped to sleep in Arkansas, and Santa Fe, New Mexico. I would drive through hail storms, and I even get a few flat tires. I was all alone, with no one to talk to. All of my life, that is how I have felt—alone. I was comfortable being alone, though, because being alone meant you were strong.

After my three-day journey was over, I arrived in Arizona excited to embark upon a new adventure. Ironically, I bumped into a college friend at a local bar out there. While in Arizona, I ran a few professional road races and finally realized my running career was over. Sports had played their purpose, and the mission accomplished banner was finally raised high. So, I now had a new job, a new place to live, and a new life post-graduation.

When I began working at the company, I met the VP of sales, Reg Givens—an African-American man who was sharp all around. I was shocked to see a man of color in such a high position, and I looked up to him. He took the time to mentor me after everyone left for the day, and I embraced every word that came out of his mouth. The way he dressed and the way he spoke was incredible.

During this time, starting my new career, I received a serious phone call from my brother. He came to visit me and have a conversation about some things I wasn't ready for. After serving time in the Marine Corp, he said he would go back into the reserves. This move into the reserves would make him eligible to enter into the Iraq war.

My brother was training in Palm Springs, California, and this visit was to discuss his Will with me. I was not ready for that conversation and was scared that maybe he wouldn't come back. I was at a loss for words when he visited me, and I remember hearing my brother tell me how proud he was of me. He said he would be deployed for eighteen months. Thank God he came home in one piece.

While working in Arizona for a year, and doing well at my job, I developed friendships that would last a long time. But when Reg sat me down in his office and let me know I was being transferred to Denver, Colorado, I was upset because I wanted to go to California or even Las Vegas! He knew what was best for me, and at the time living in either one of those places was not in my best interest.

"Jesus Calling"

This world is so cruel how do we love
At times it so hard, no presence of a beautiful white dove
The man above transformed my path
Now I have enemies coming at me with vengeance and wrath
I stay focused and sometimes even laugh
Not even my wounds can endure this sea salt bath
All the pain I feel today
I look up to the sky, no blue, just gray
Can I sail far, or should I stay at bay
Reminiscing the days where it was all good and sunny like May
Lord will you hold my hand through this wicked land
Or am I helpless like a yearning old man
What is our purpose and what is your plan
Is it not enough that I am a surviving fan
Since I have followed you my enemies are real
My pain so deep I wish I could heal
Are my words right or am I falling
On my knees wishing for Jesus Calling

CHAPTER 9

THE MILE-HIGH CITY

The first time I came to Colorado, I was amazed by the natural beauty and how clean it was everywhere. At the time, it was still a small city. Legalization of marijuana would soon change that. I would move to the Denver Tech Center and fall in love immediately with the city. It was home, and I knew this is where I wanted to settle down.

When I got to Denver, life was good. I was making six figures, and the cost of living was pretty cheap. Rumors of a market collapse were consistently in the news, but our executives would assure us that we, as a company, were okay. Except one day I would wake up and suddenly find myself going from a six-figure income to being unemployed.

The financial meltdown was really due to subprime loans defaulting at a high rate. What was I to do in a new city with no job? To make matters worse, I found out that my girlfriend from college was pregnant, and a baby was on the way. My back was against the wall, and I decided to marry her. At the time, I pursued being a stock broker but had difficulty passing the Series 7 test. Yellowpages.com contacted me for an interview for selling online advertising, and that would be the door I needed to go through to get back on my feet.

I was very rough around the edges and a little bit cocky. I thought my interview went well, but I would later find out they didn't want to hire me. I was not mature and had a bit of a southern ascent. Ms. Amy and LeAndre would give me an opportunity of a lifetime, and I wouldn't let them down. We were responsible for memorizing a four page script for the first day of training. If you failed, you were sent home immediately after two tries. Chris Parker, Mike Pisa, and David Carlson would stay up with me all night to make sure I got it done.

Yellowpages.com was owned by AT&T, and our job was to get businesses on the online directory to transition from the paper phone book. I started off as an entry level sales rep and went on to be promoted four times until finally, I was making up to 250,000 dollars a year as an executive.

My mentor at the company, LeAndre Baily, took me under his wing and mentored me from day one. He invested countless hours in my growth, and as he went up the ladder, I followed right behind him. Ironically he was an African American male, just like Reg, and was a lot older than I was. I soaked up everything he taught me and had his back. I worked long hours and was obsessed. The same drive and work ethic I had for athletics I applied to corporate America. I saw the politics, the bias, the racism, the good, the bad, and the ugly.

I had two strikes against me: one was my age; the other was the fact that I didn't look like everyone else. In addition to that, I didn't communicate like everyone else either. I was very raw with words. But after two years in sales, I was promoted as a district sales manager and ran a small team of ten reps. I would often get on the phones with my team and run in the trenches right beside them. I knew the job well because I was a top sales rep and earned the presidential club honors. As a district manager, I went on to run one of the best teams in the company.

My teams were always diverse, and I always made sure they were balanced with males and females. The secret to my success was simple. Lead by example and earn your respect as a leader.

After four years, I was promoted to General Manager and ran a team of thirty plus reps responsible for over twelve million dollars in revenue. Money was great, and all the material things that came with it were also great, but I was not happy deep inside. I was living a double life, and I wanted out of my marriage. I wanted out of the pain of not knowing who I was.

Instead, I would continue to buy bigger houses and better cars to mask the pain. I would travel and work more hours to run from reality. The reality was that I never stopped to deal with my childhood. I never stopped to deal with the pain of my father and the pain of my mother. I never released the internal pain of my childhood. Instead, I isolated my thoughts and made reckless decisions in order to cope with the pain. This meant lying, cheating on my wife, and even ignoring her emotions.

By this time, I had two beautiful daughters. I always made time for them and loved them dearly. My girls have always been the center of my universe. But as the success came, so did more mistakes in my personal life. On one hand, I was a well-respected business man; and on the other hand, I was a lonely man, lost and confused. Only my inner circle knew both men. No one else. At some point, I saw the ending coming fast, and I knew it would be catastrophic. But until then, I had to keep living the lie and living the so-called American dream.

CHAPTER 10

ITALY, WHERE IT ALL BEGAN

At the peak of my reign as an executive and business man, I decided to take my immediate family and my mother to Italy to discover where it all began. We traveled to Venice, Florence, Pisa, Tuscany, Rome, and finish our trip in Sicily to meet our family. My mother and I went a period of time without talking, and my ex and I were just about done. Regardless, the trip, in my eyes, was the fulfillment of a lifelong dream. I felt like I was learning about who I truly was. My daughters would get a trip of a lifetime, and even my mother could get a gift from a son who, at times, questioned her life.

The country was beautiful, and the art was amazing. We saw the David statue in Florence, walked the streets of Rome, visited the Vatican, ate the finest food in Tuscany, and embraced the Italian culture. I knew at that very moment that I'd made it in life, and that no one could take this from me. I had set out to do what everyone said was impossible, and this was the icing on the cake. I was grateful for this trip, even though it was not romantic with my spouse and was awkward at times with my mother. It was all about my daughters and showing them where we'd come from. When I am long gone, they will always remember their daddy taking them to Italy.

There were moments when love did show up. We attended a cooking class and took walks together. We made the best out of a situation ending. This trip defined the beginning to an end—the end of my family and a new beginning with Christ. God spoke to me through the art, and He spoke to me throughout the trip. He was real, and me stepping foot on Italian soil only proved that He was real. A skinny kid from Connecticut, who'd grown up in a small town of forty thousand people without knowing his father, with bad grades, facing extreme adversity, made it. He'd proven everyone wrong and truly beat the odds! Italy represented the pinnacle of my success.

The country of Italy was a turning point in my life because I knew that I could do anything I wanted if I put my mind to it. When I entered into the village of Mellie and walked the streets of my grandfather and met my beautiful family, it all made sense. We were a family of survivors and hard workers. I grew a great appreciation for what my grandfather and grandmother created. He traveled thousands of miles with no guarantees, no perfect conclusions. He left his home country for a better life and a better future for his family. He sacrificed everything to provide a future for his children, and I admired that so much. He was an honorable man, and my grandmother was an honorable woman. They were cut from a different cloth. I would learn on that trip what honor was really about. Sacrifice, hard work, dedication, and risk would define my thought process moving forward.

Unfortunately, my grandparents were no longer alive to know that we'd traveled to their country. I lost my grandfather in high school and my grandmother while I was in college to suicide. They were smiling down from heaven while we were out there, and I know it.

"Jesus Spoke to Me"

I closed my eyes and entered a dream
Suddenly I was running and heard uncontrollable screams
Everything we had was going away
I looked up at the sky and yes it was grey
Our old house and even the cars were on fire
Yelling and screaming of those calling me a horrible liar
All the money was gone from the bank
My eyes were open I couldn't even blink
Until one day, we walked in the church
We heard a message about putting God first
All of a sudden, things began to change
The sky's turned blue which seemed so strange
Hundreds and thousands of struggling people listened
to our story of pain
Jesus entered the room and insisted no one was to blame
The things we held on to were not all true
He also said materialism is a sickness like the flu
All of us sat and listened while he smiled for miles
No longer was I in deliberate denial
I realized that our past life doesn't represent who we truly are
Jesus continued to walk, and we saw him from a far
We yelled for His attention and made one final plea
An elder man would suddenly enter the dream
Looked into my eyes and said not to worry because
"Jesus spoke to Me."

CHAPTER 11

FINDING JESUS

After years of running from the Lord, I entered His house, got on my knees, and begged for His mercy. I surrendered my soul, and the double life had finally ended. I would be introduced to men's groups and even serving others through our food bank. I finally found my purpose in life—serving others in need. I learned through scripture that you can't serve two gods. Money and God don't mix. From that point on, I had one God.

I went to church every single Sunday and opened up in groups, sharing my story of pain. I hadn't grown up in the church, so all of this was brand new. I was a new man overnight. Just like that, with God's help. At least I thought so. Some people didn't buy into the Jesus Tom, though. In my journey, I'd hurt a lot of people, and they were not going for it.

I learned how to be faithful taking an eight week purity class, and I learned how to forgive. This didn't mean I was perfect and mistake free. When I found Jesus, I want to be clear that I was not perfect with my attitude or all of my decisions. At this point, I now had a conscious. I cared now, and I was willing to be vulnerable with my soul. I was now free from the pain and used my pain as a tool to help other men who struggled with what I'd struggled with.

My daughters found Jesus right alongside with me, and we invited him into our hearts. Not everyone around us subscribed to this, though, and I will just leave it at that. My life didn't get easier when I found Jesus, although most people think it should. Jesus is not Santa Claus. He stripped me of all my idols one by one—my house, my cars, my wife, and even my money. It all went away because the Lord wanted to make sure this was real.

My ex-wife filed for divorce after I transformed, and the house went next. Then I got laid off from my job too before my divorce finalized. I spent thousands of dollars in divorce court and wiped out my entire savings. Everything was gone! Just like that, my empire was flattened. I had no one to blame but myself. Through the process, I am grateful for God's mercy on my soul. This was the moment in my life that I needed. If I could make every single mistake again, I would. I had to go through it and learn the hard way. Unfortunately, I hurt good people, and that part I regret.

Baptism would follow next, and my continuation of serving would follow daily. I began to live off no money, but I was living my life with more purpose. God now had His hand on my shoulder, and I felt safe—plus I felt a freedom from His love. Many people criticized my walk with Jesus, and more enemies would emerge behind the curtains. I wasn't concerned or focused on the negativity.

My life had changed, and so had I. God knew that the man I used to be had died and was six feet under. Finding Jesus was not a fad; it was a new way of life.

Again, did this mean I was perfect? Absolutely not. I had many flaws still, but now I had a clear understanding of how to live my life. I learned how to deal with temptation and lust through countless hours of groups. Every man, I believe, has these issues deep down inside. God has stripped me down to blood and bones and has radically transformed my mind. As scripture would illustrate in John, Chapter 8, Jesus would heal a blind man from being blind. He would spit in the dirt to make mud and put the mud on the man's eyes. After growing up blind, the man would be healed. All of the people who witnessed this miracle would see the blind man as the same man, a beggar and a disabled man, even though the man who was healed from Jesus's touch. I found similarity in that story with my own. I was healed from Jesus's touch, but many of my adversaries only saw the old me.

I went on to volunteer at the food bank and shelters, joined a men's group, became a public speaker to our youth, coached youth basketball teams, and many other things to follow Christ. Praise God for touching my heart and soul.

CHAPTER 12

GIANNA AND AVA'S FATHER

As my transformation was coming to light, so, too, was my impact on my two beautiful daughters. I had joint custody of them, and I made sure I was getting them ready for life as an adult. Our cadence was precise and sometimes too much, if you ask others. We volunteered together at food banks, shelters, karate, basketball, kumon, and praised the Lord every Sunday that I had them in my custody.

Gianna was falling in love with basketball, so a lot of her energy was going into that sport. I began to head coach her rec team after being an assistant coach for many years. Ava was the complete opposite and had a huge personality. Her ambition was dance and being known by all. In the classroom, Gianna had a gift to learn and was in gifted courses. Ava didn't take too much to school on the academic side of things but was popular throughout the school. Gianna would go on to be selected in Spelling Bees and also attend student council. I don't really know how the girls took to the divorce, but they would always ask me whether I would ever get back with their mother.

We had strict rules at my house in regards to sleepovers or the girls going to someone else's house. I didn't allow it because I valued my time with them. I can't speak of what they did when they weren't at my house, but I know one thing: when they were with me, we focused on education, self-defense, healthy activities and God.

When I didn't have my daughters, I would fall into a deep depression at home alone. Yes, I dated women from time to time, but it just wasn't the same when I didn't have my daughters. All I ever wanted to be was an excellent father because of the pain my father had caused me. I wanted them to know every single second on this planet that their daddy loved them. I made a lot of mistakes in my adult life, but being a father was never one of them. I enjoyed and took great pride in being a father. The folks I hurt would never give me credit for being a great dad, and I was okay with that because I would just use that negative energy to be even better.

I save all the tickets and memorable items we share, so one day they can look back at all that we did. Every six months, we take family pictures to illustrate our family love. When I was married, I always wanted to do that, but unfortunately, we never got around to doing it. We all pray together as a family every single night, and our prayers always bring a tear to my eyes. My daughters are growing up so fast, and one day, they finally asked the question: "Daddy, why did Mommy divorce you?" I broke down and cried as we walked to the car after watching a heartfelt movie. I prayed before answering them and told them the truth. "Your mommy divorced me because Daddy was not being a good husband, and I couldn't stop cheating on her." That was the truth, and it took everything and my spirit to deliver that message. I'd let them down, and I saw it in their faces. They didn't ask why, they just looked at me as if they knew it was wrong. I didn't get into making up excuses or blaming their mother. Sure, blame can always be used as a scapegoat, but I was a different man.

The drive home that night was silent and hurtful, but it was necessary. My actions did not reflect the man I truly was, and I knew that. After our divorce, although I would go on to date a few women, I never cheated again. Cheating is so bad, and I wish I'd enough courage in my past life to be a real man. When we go our entire lives acting out and doing the wrong thing, it's hard to recognize our faults and bad habits. Almost like smoking a cigarette— everyone who smokes knows it's bad but for some reason they keep on doing it.

My number one priority as a single dad was being a great father, and it took me a considerable amount of time to overcome the thought of failure with my divorce. I was embarrassed and ashamed of my previous actions. That lead to my divorce, as a husband, I flat out failed and had no one to blame but myself.

Gianna and Ava continue to grow and be their own individuals. Like most sisters, they fight, they play, and they fight some more. I was inspired to write this book because of them. When I leave this precious Earth, I want them to know who their dad truly is. I am not a saint, but

I am a man who put them first and loved people. Most men give up on their children, and now I understand why. As a man, you have many pressures from the world, and my challenge has always been co-parenting. How can two people agree on anything when you go through an emotional divorce? How can two people agree on anything when both people see the world completely different? I now understand why my father and many other fathers walk away. It is a lot to deal with a woman who hates you and deal with an environment that is so toxic.

Let me be crystal clear. I don't condone men who walk away. In fact, I disagree with it 100%. However, I understand the pain, and I understand the decision based on my own personal experience. There were times when I thought about walking away, and I thank God I did not. I wonder about people when they say, I can't believe that man or woman cheated on their significant other. Or what a bad man or woman for making that decision. Here is my thought about those judgmental statements we all have. Unless we have lived in that person's shoes, how can we judge a man or woman? As Jesus said in the Bible, he who is free from sin cast the first stone—while in the presence of men who wanted to stone a woman for committing adultery. Let us be careful not to judge—especially if we are not free from sin.

CHAPTER 13

DIVORCE

I failed. Yes, for the first time in my life, I looked into the mirror and said it out loud. I failed at my marriage. There is no one to blame but myself. The only people who win in a divorce are the lawyers and the haters. My ex-wife and I created an empire from scratch, and many people waited and waited for it all to come crashing down. To this day, I have my opinions and my theories, but for the sake of my soul, I will take all the blame. One of the most painful experiences in my life was being served papers that ended my immediate family as I knew it.

Thousands of dollars were spent on legal fees, my dream house gone, my children gone half the time out of my life, my car gone, my job gone, my 401K gone completely, and everything I'd worked for over a ten-year period, gone! God opened my eyes to many things through these times. He taught me that money is truly evil, and how you idolize it will affect you dramatically. I would later have a conversation with my brother, Alex, on the topic of divorce. I asked him what was harder: serving a tour in the Iraq war or going through a divorce. He answered, "A divorce!"

No matter all the things I did right while married—such as being a great provider, helping others in my family, going to work every day, and many, many other things that were positive—it didn't matter one bit. Every great deed I ever did as a married man would become blemished. Family members called me a bad man, a liar, a monster, and other demeaning things. I fell into the deepest depression as a result and fell in love with sleeping my shame away. I stayed in bed while unemployed for twenty hours some days just to cope with the pain. Depression is real, and it came for my soul with a wicked vengeance.

Who could I run to in this dark period of my life? Jesus was the only person who listened to my pain. He is the only one that provided mercy. Job was also a man who had many things, which he would lose. Through this trial and tribulation, I learned there is beauty in suffering. The humility I faced going from a Mercedes to a Dodge Caravan with 200,000 miles on it was real. God was teaching me a great lesson in all of this—material things, and even love, aren't real sometimes. His love mattered, and so did His forgiveness.

I fell in love with scripture through this dark time and also became an advocate to save other marriages. As I have shared with those who struggle in their marriage, divorce is not a solution. I advise against divorce because your family is one of God's greatest gifts on this planet. The devil hates family, and he hates unity. Being single is not fun because those who are single are always searching for stability.

I am asked this same question over and over again about remarrying. At first, I said no way, but now I have matured in that thought. Yes, I would marry again. Marriage is a beautiful thing, but you have to embrace it and lean in to it knowing that it is a journey. I wasn't ready for marriage one bit, and I knew it the day I got married. My marriage failed before it even started. In order to have a successful marriage, I believe that you need honesty, communication, trust, love, values, morals, patience, passion, fear, joy, and laughter.

Divorce is such a nasty action because it will leave an everlasting scar on your soul. Those who convince you of divorce are not your friends or better, yet they do not love you at all. Now in cases of violence, or other abusive circumstances there are exceptions. In my opinion it is not the place of another to motivate the breaking up of a family. Breaking up a family is worse than being strung out on drugs. Divorce destroys the make-up of your kids because your kids have to live with the aftermath of the devastation. The kids suffer the most, and the anger and hate resumes years later. Divorced couples learn to hate each other intensely for years.

In high school and college, students should take a mandatory class on marriage and divorce. I now know why 50% of married couples don't last because for some reason, people think divorce is the solution to a miserable marriage. This is inaccurate and far from the truth. When you marry someone, the expectation is that the other person will make you happy! Happiness is only generated through your own free will. No man or woman can provide you with happiness. This is not at all possible. We all go into a marriage with this expectation, and when it doesn't happen, we hit the eject button.

Human beings are so obsessed with feelings. Feelings are great servants and horrible masters. Our feelings lead us down a lonely, dark hole with no happy ending. How you feel is so irrelevant because in this lifetime, outcomes matter most. If you knew your kids would suffer, your finances would suffer, your health would suffer, your security would suffer, and most importantly you will suffer, would you invest in that direction? Probably not. Leaving your partner does not guarantee you happiness. Divorce is an evil reality that most won't talk about.

This chapter was the hardest for me to write, and I hope you understand the pain from these words. Don't do it because the grass isn't greener on the other side; the grass is greener where you water it.

The Sun Shines Bright

What will you do when you become welcomed and renewed
Will you flourish or continue to be stuck like glue
Those that hate you will not go away
If you want to succeed focus on work, not play
Have a structured balance and put God first
Know your true value, know your worth
The world will truly see you how you are
Never look back or worry about how far
Love is the light you will someday seek
Strength is in forgiveness that doesn't mean your weak
God blesses the peacemakers and undoubtingly the meek
Keep your head up never look to your feet
Let my words guide you in to a season of wealth
Focus on your attitude, invest in your health
When a person points at you don't worry if their right
Pray to God frequently that tomorrow the Sun Shines Bright

CHAPTER 14

A NEW PURPOSE

After losing my job, family, cars, house, and money, I refocused my life on serving other people. Could I have gone out and made big money and been the corporate guy again right away? Sure. But God's purpose for me was to help others with their pain. I saw what idolizing money can do to your soul. I saw what living an ungodly life provides. It is an empty life. It is a painful life because you are always chasing something that is not real. Jesus preached about servitude and helping others in need, and now I finally got it. This life isn't about us, and it isn't about how many cars you buy. This life is about our deeds, our love towards others, and our servitude heart.

Being a rich man has nothing to do with money. Being a rich man has everything to do with how you think. If money defined wealth, you could take $100 to a third world country and be well off for a month. My advice to you is this: Every day you wake up, listen to your heart. What is it telling you to do? Take away how much you will earn, and all the feelings and emotions wrapped around the thought. God will always provide clarity when you seek His help.

At a young age, I made a covenant with God. I told Him that if he released me from my childhood, I would give back to those who walked a similar path. I would lead by example—not by winning all the time but by having the courage to fail. In my life, my failures have brought me to greater places than my successes. We are taught that losing is bad and losing is shameful. In contrast, losing is necessary—to WIN! If we don't know how to lose, we will never know how to win, and that is a fact of life, in my opinion.

You see, growing up a certain race, from a city or small town, abused or not abused, healthy or sick, happy or sad, or even rich or poor, we are all born to suffer and succeed. In this life, not one man is free from pain or suffering. That is the great equalizer in humanity—pain. How we deal with it is another thing we cope with. Some of us get high, and others will be motivated to be successful. How will you utilize your adversity, and how will you embrace your suffering? Will you run and run and run some more? Or will you face it on head on and allow it to free you? Almost my entire adult life, I ran and hid from my secrets and past. I compiled my dirt under the biggest rug I could find. Eventually, the dirt becomes a mound, and everyone begins to see the lump under your rug. Uncover the dirt and free yourself from self-shame and pain. No man on this planet has the authority to judge you or to criticize you. God knows our heart and soul, and being honest and free from our pain makes our life that much better.

Today, my bank account isn't as large as I want it to be, and my material things don't bling bling, but my faith and servitude are massive. I have recommitted my life to the struggle, and now I am honest about my past. I know who I am, and that tells me who I am not. Some of us don't know who we are, and in turn we act out on who we are not. Our time on this Earth is very short—so short that when you look up, it will all be over. How will we be remembered? What will future generations say about us long after we are gone? That is what pushes me to be the best person—my legacy. I want to live on forever and ever in a positive light.

CHAPTER 15

THE DEVIL IS A LIAR

"Submit yourselves therefore to God. Resist the devil and he will flee from you" (James 4:7).

When you understand the devil and you understand how he works, your life will become easier. Satan is the father of lies. He is most interested in your mind. He doesn't care about your money, your material things—only your mind. When your mind is lost, so are your actions. He blinds the minds of unbelievers with evil thoughts. He will make you believe there is no God, and how can there be a God if negative things happen. We must know that God is not Santa Claus. He is a God of love but also through our adversity and suffering, we grow inside. For example, losing my job, family, and certain friends have altered my thought process so that I can be a better man. It put my servitude high on my priority scale.

The devil tempts us all into sin because all sin leads to death. He causes sickness and disease through our negative thoughts. Our families are one of our biggest assets on this planet outside of our faith in God. While I was married, the devil put in front of me what my biggest weaknesses were. He gave me an abundant amount of money to destroy myself. He encouraged me to idolize money because on every Internet site, all the pictures represent money. All the pictures on TV we see are signals sometimes used by this evil creator. That's why scripture helps us to fight his wicked ways.

A lot of unbelievers will say things like church going people are hypocrites because they believe one thing and do another. Let me be clear: following Jesus does not qualify anyone to be perfect. We strive to walk with God, but as humans, we will fail and at times lose control because we walk in the flesh. Since I have been walking with Christ, an enormous number of people have doubted my faith and criticized my walk. I have learned to embrace this simply because my walk is with Him, not with the human race. When we learn to please God, great blessings will happen, indeed. We can never please another human being. That is not our job. The devil understands our flaws a lot better than we do. He believes in divorce, death, lies, pain, and manipulation.

Looking back at my flaws, I see where the devil was right by my side. At times it bothers me because I can't believe I was so weak. Most children make mistakes growing up, and when we are weak in faith, we show up as a child who simply doesn't know best. To be free in Christ means that you are not ashamed of your past. You don't hide who you were. We have all been forgiven by God, and He died for our sins. The voices you hear in your head are real voices because some come from God and others do come from the devil. The greatest gift God gives us is choice. We have a loving God who allows mankind to make our own decisions—decisions to love, decisions to kill, decisions to help others, and the decisions to do right. We are not victims of circumstances. We are outcomes of circumstances. However, a second chance is a new opportunity to make it right and to do right.

I wanted to spend time expressing to you the significance of evil and the devil because he is around us every day through media outlets, through violence, through hate, through the Internet, and many other tools he uses. When we have God in our hearts, the devil has no room to manipulate and destroy us.

LORD CAN YOU HEAR ME

My enemies attack me with anger and lies
You are giving me patience and making me wise
The devil sits by my bed and waits for me to wake
All my money is gone Lord, now what more can he take
When I close my eyes, you instruct me to stay on course
And to stop worrying about my meaningless divorce
My deeds shine bright and the way I lead as a father
Keep on praying says the Lord, He is protecting my daughters
When the dust settles your enemies will be gone
Those that follow Satan will be proven wrong
Put on God's armor, fight don't flee
On my knees at night asking, Lord can you hear Me

CHAPTER 16

MOVING ON IN GOD'S GRACE

Looking forward to the future, I see so much—someday walking my daughters down the aisle, high school and college graduations, being a grandfather, falling back in love, and continuing to walk right beside God. My life has truly been a blessing, and I am forever grateful for God's grace. Beating the odds is what my life has been about since day one. As I said before, I am not a perfect man, but I've learned in life that it doesn't matter what people call you, it only matters what you respond to. I love all my enemies and those that wish on my downfall.

This book is dedicated to all those who have faced adversity and think there is no light at the end of the tunnel. God hears your prayers, and He feels your pain. Just hang in there. Remember one thing: pain is temporary. It may last a day, a week, or even a year, but be assured of one thing: it won't last forever.

Writing this book has allowed me to feel inner peace and reflect on a life of struggle and pain. Many people came into my life for a reason and a purpose. I fully understand the why now. How will you live your life? Will you live it in anger, or in peace? It's your choice, and God gives you that choice. Every day I wake up I understand my purpose; it is to help others achieve in this life. As Jesus did with His life, so, too, will I do with mine. He lived His life for others even until His final breath. My purpose is crystal clear now. I will focus my efforts on positive energy, period. If someone isn't giving off positive energy and not praying for me and encouraging me to be great, then I don't need them around me. Everything coming out of my mouth from this day forward has to be positive.

Evil Won't Prevail

Screams and cries of what he did
Who cares that he was sexually abused as a kid
And who cares about his pain
When everything fails we need someone to blame
Behind closed doors they want to see us dead
Isn't it crazy for years I provided wine and bread
How can you hate someone for an unlimited time?
The person sinned but never committed a crime
Jesus said he who hasn't sinned cast the first stone
You got what u wanted now to leave me alone
Hate is wicked and so is the tongue
Will you be happy if there is a public execution
showing me hung
On my knees I admit I failed
Lastly know this evil won't prevail

CHAPTER 17

RECOVERY

Depression, anxiety, shame, withdraw, animosity, and many other symptoms happen when we decide not to get help. Thank God my support systems were in play when I found Jesus. These include men's groups, celebrate recovery (healing group), church, fellowships, self-help courses, coaching, public speaking, authoring this book, and surrounding myself with positive energy. I also removed all negative people from my life immediately. When the money went away, most of my so-called friends vanished. I could count on two hands how many friends and family I could trust.

When you start following Christ, He will reveal to you a different reality. While I was recovering, I would hear the whispers of my transformation being labeled as show. After two years of consistently getting help, I would laugh and say this is an awful long show! When you are doing positive and doing right, the attacks will become abundant. The reason being is that most people fall in love with the shameful person you once were. It allows them to feel superior. Former loved ones will make sure all their friends still see you as a monster while they play the victim. I believe that no one is a victim on this planet. We are human beings with circumstances—some good, some bad—but we all have a choice. If you don't like something or someone, discontinue it. If you decide to put up with bad behavior for years, are you really a victim? My recovery revealed to me who I am and who I am not. I am a good man, a good father, and I care about people. In addition to that, my past life doesn't represent who I am today. Also, it does not define who I am. Those whom I hurt will convince themselves of that, unfortunately.

I see the world differently today. How could I be the same person after losing a two hundred and fifty-thousand-dollar job, my wife, my kids half the time, my cars, my dream house, my money, and my dignity? The ironic fact is that I changed before I lost everything. Let me be clear: the minute I started following Christ was I 100% perfect, NO. When people follow Jesus Christ, it seems to be an opportunity for people to hold you to an unrealistic standard. If you go to church you still bleed, you still get sick, you still go through a yellow light. Through my recovery stage, I learned how to be faithful and also how to love unconditionally. We can learn how to gravitate towards sex, drugs, and even eating when we suffer. Pain is real, and we all want to feel good. How are you investing your time, and how are you growing from yesterday? I constantly ask myself that on a daily basis.

After being stripped down to bone, I started to obsess about having a family and even getting married again.

Why not? Now I know how to do it effectively. I had a few close calls, but unfortunately those relationships did not materialize. At this point, I am continuing to serve others and fall back in love with myself. The number one priority in my life outside of God is making sure my daughters become great women. Being a single dad is very challenging, but I wouldn't trade it in for anything. With less money now and fewer material things, I still have double compared to what I had before. My circle is tight. I don't have anyone around me acting ungodly. Everyone around me is considered a mentor or someone who is giving off positive energy in my life.

Let's face it, every now and then someone will show up in my life with a great story line and then get exposed. The beauty of following God is that He will give you vision. The devil is very misleading, so be careful of what you think is real. During your recovery, it is very important to acknowledge who you hurt and make sure you communicate to them your remorse. The minute after my divorce, I wrote those I had hurt, and hopefully they are reading this sentence in my book to verify in their head this act I conducted. One of the hardest things I have ever had to do was write those letters of sincerity to them. However, after I did so the shame was removed because now it was in God's hands. At times all we can do is apologize and move on. We cannot alter the way folks feel about us. In fact, it is impossible—that's why we release it to God's hands. Don't spend your life trying to hope others see you differently. Follow God and keep your eyes on Him.

The word *recover* does not mean you are completely fixed. When you recover, you are healing from a wound that affected you and affected others. It will not be overnight that all the pain goes away. While on this path, others will still judge you and try to hurt you. Stay focused on God and God only through this process. As I write these words, I know that I am still recovering from the pain. Please put all your faith in God, and you will be free.

CHAPTER 18

THE ODDS

1.8% of High School Athletes make it to a Division 1 College from High School in Track & Field. Source: NCAA.org

1.8% of High School Athletes make it to a Division 1 College from High School in Cross Country. Source: NCAA.org

5.4% of Americans make six figure incomes. Source: U.S. Census

40% of working-aged Americans hold a college degree. Source: Lumina Foundation

1 in 100 million sperm fertilize a female egg. Source: https://www.webmd.com/

40% of college students make it to graduation. Source: https://www.collegeraptor.com/

60% of college students drop out. Source: https://www.collegeraptor.com/

17% of custodial single parents are men. Source: https://www.fatherhood.gov/content/dad-stats

CHAPTER 19

THANK YOU

High School Diploma
All-Conference XC MEAC Conf 00,01,02
All-Conference MEAC Outdoor Track 00,01,02
President of Phi Delta Psi Kappa Chapter 01-02
Bachelor's Degree Interdisciplinary Studies
Father Gianna Hightower (2007)
and Ava Hightower (2010)
Basketball Coach for Aurora Rec
National public speaker
Author
Activist
Executive Yellowpages.com at age of 30
Won 3 Winners Circle awards for YP.com
Traveled to Italy with my daughters,
ex-wife, and mother (2015)
Bought my dream house on Algonquian Cir
Bought my dream car, 2016 E350 Mercedes Benz
Made over 6-figure income for 10 straight years in a row
Found a men's Christian group, July 2016 to present

Found Jesus Christ, May 2016
Presently at Peace

Thank you to all the people in my life who said I couldn't make it out of Connecticut. Thank you to all the people who had an opinion of me as a man and as a kid. Thank you to all the people who said I couldn't go division one because I went to high school in a small town. Thank you to all the people who said I was crazy and wasn't a good father. Thank you to all the people who said I couldn't manage on a corporate level because I was too young and inexperienced. Thank you to all the people who prayed my marriage wouldn't last and all my material things would go away. Thank you to all the people who judged me before even knowing my story. Thank you for all the so-called friends and girlfriends who said they loved me and left my side while I was battling my depression. Thank you to all the people who told me I would never write a book and be an author. Thank you to certain family members who abandoned me when I needed them most—please know I forgive you and still love you.

Thank you to all the teachers who said I could be anything I set out to be if I worked hard and put my mind to it. Thank you to my true friends, who never gave up on me no matter who I was. Thank you to my daughters for coming into this Earth and loving me every single second of the day. Thank you to all the corporations that gave me a shot to earn a living and teaching me that we still have a long way to go for workplace equality. Thank you to my church home, Smoky Hill Vineyard, for opening their doors when no one was around to help me through a dark period of my life. Thank you to my older brother for being a role model and a man for me to look up to. Thank you to my mother and Eddie Hightower for meeting and bringing me into this world. Thank you to my mother especially for sacrificing and doing her very best. Thank you to my stepfather Tim for doing the best he could as a parent and supporting my mother and family. Thank you to my sisters for always loving me and having my back. Thank you to the Balanceau family for being a second family to me growing up and present. Thank you to the town of Stafford Springs and all the parents I didn't mention, and Connecticut for loving me. Thank you to Norfolk State University, Norfolk, Virginia, and the seven cities for helping me to become a man. Thank you to all the mentors I have had in my life who supported me through everything—Steve Levinthal, Karen Fair, Clint Santoro, Coach Floyd Conley, Coach Giles, Coach Gary Baker, Reg Givens, LeAndre Bailey, and Pirro Kocci.

Lastly, thank you to my Lord Jesus Christ for radically transforming my life.

Thank you for reading my story, and hopefully you took at least one thing from that will help you to become a better person. I love you from the bottom of my heart!

THE END

I gave my best at this thing called life
When it is all over who cares who is wrong or right
We learn how to win strong and how to fight
Most of the time we get sucked into the negative hype
This is my story and I am sticking to it
No fancy illusions or sudden tricks
Some loved me for me and others hated my soul
Throughout my life I always understood my unique role
Love and respect is all I ever seek
God blesses the humble and even the meek
When the lies and deception came I had to turn the other cheek
It doesn't mean I was unfit or even weak
How will the generations echo my forgotten name
Will it come with glory or will I still to come to blame
My goal was for my little girls to know their daddies real life
Hopefully one day I remarry and find a Godly wife
So many people blessed me with their precious time
Finding the next word to utter hoping it rhymes
At the very end we must be flexible and even bend
Thank you for listening and making it to the end

"If God is For Me, Who can Be Against Me"

ACKNOWLEDGMENTS

Special thanks to: Jesus Christ, my Lord and Savior; Gianna and Ava Hightower; Auntie Phil; Grandma and Grandpa Sgarellino; Nellie Hudson (my mother); Eddie Hightower; Alex Williams; Christine Hudson; Tim Hudson; Jen Hudson; the entire Balanceau family; Stafford Springs, Connecticut; Mad Money M; Big TJ (RIP); Mike Ference (RIP) and family; Aaron Moore (RIP); Coach Kenneth Giles; Floyd Conley (RIP); Phi Delta Psi Fraternity; Steven Leventhal (RIP) and his entire family; Clint Santoro; Norfolk State University; Mike Temple; Dwayne Kendrick; Donte Lucas; Norman Forrest; Dr. Joey Rosario; Ms. Cynthia Lewis; Leandre Bailey; Reginald Givens; Shelly and Jason Hightower; Dorthy Hightower; Karen Fair; Frank McNulty; Pat Eastburn; Shane Bornstein; Lisa Zielinski; Tyrona Heath; Lopez Lomong; Christopher Brown; Kellie Wells; the entire Norfolk State Track and cross country team's men and women (2000–2005); Ray Young; Mark Young and family; Kirk Stewart; B. Nathaniel Smith; Harry Chin;

Sharon Miller; Mike Casinelli; Adam Casinelli and his family; Angela Dickerson; Marlon Williams; Morgan and Steven; Jamie Poe; Brandon Prescott; Sharif Dyson; Ed Grant and his entire family; Anthony Attalla; Isaac Cruz and family; Justin Kaufman; Flonzo Perry; Mark Dunn; Francis Kennedy; Danny Deal; Barbra McCoy; Ms. Yolanda; Greg Stephenson; Aurora Rec; John Mayo and family; Joven Luca and family; Patrice Reynolds; Corinne Rucker; Pirro Kocci; Tami Johnson; KG; Slick Rick Hernandez; Harry Jones; Jeffrey Easley; Dennis Jones; all the founders of PDPSI; Lee Bailey; Tony Lampkin; Glenn Harris; Jamie Dickson; Shawn Baboval, Valerie Baboval, and family; Jerome Ballard and family; BN; P. Lua; Tupac and Biggie; Mario Avila and everyone at Big Thinkers Media; Yellowpages.com; Kay Jewelers; Tyrone Ashford and his entire family; TyTy: all the Woodards from Bloomfield; SF; T Hall and his entire family; ATL family; VA family; the twins Dione and Darrnel; Seneca; ACE; Gary Baker, my first coach; the Dreish family; Vicky, Pat, and Corey; Todd Binnette and family; Clint Talbot and his entire family; Winston Aberdeen; Lt. Price NSU; Ebony Jones; David Carlson; Mike Pisa; Chris Parker; Kenny and Barry Adams; Andrew CT;Amy Hegarty; Tyrona Heath; Jamie Dickson; Seve Irv; all my relatives from Italy; Tony Flint and his entire family; Jason and Shelly Hightower; Dorothy Hightower; Mike Adams; Tom Lynch and my entire men's group; Darin, Nakia Garret; Eny and Natalie Gomez; Brian and Steve Tone and their entire family; Olaf A.; John Lee; Elmer S.; Nick C; Suheil; Pace and his entire family; Moses Brewer and family; Charles Pankey and his entire family; and Justin Lewis; Dale and Kay Gaston; Derick McCarty and family, Chaz and Teresa Edmonds, Greg Thompson Pastor Smoky Hill Vineyard and his entire family.

If I forgot your name, I am sorry. Many people had a huge influence on my life. Please know leaving you off this list was not intentional at all.